Immigration and Asylum

IRIS TEICHMANN

FRANKLIN WATTS
LONDON•SYDNEY

First published in 2002 by Franklin Watts
96 Leonard Street, London EC2A 4XD

Franklin Watts Australia
56 O'Riordan Street
Alexandria, NSW 2015

Copyright © Franklin Watts 2002

Series editor: Rachel Cooke
Series design: White Design
Picture research: Diana Morris

A CIP catalogue record for this book is available from the British Library.

ISBN 0 7496 4437 0

Dewey Classification 323.8

Printed in Belgium

Acknowledgements:
Whilst every attempt has been made to clear copyright should there be any inadvertent
omission please apply in the first instance to the publisher regarding rectification.
Pietden Blanken/Panos: 13b. Ed Carreon/Rex Features: 4t.
Martha Cooper/Stll Pictures: 24b. Matias Costa/Panos: 16b.
Howard Davies/Exile Images: 11t, 15t, 26t. H van Denberg/Rex Features: 5b.
C. Harris/Rex Features: 8. Pete Jones/Photofusion: 25t.
Lorpresse/Sygma/Corbis: 15b, 26b. Sasse Martin/Corbis: 20b.
Museum of the City of New York/Burt G Phillips/Hulton Archive: 6b.
Thomas Raupach/Still Pictures: front cover, 9b. Rex Features: 23b, 27b.
Dominic Ridley/Still Pictures: 22t. J Russell/Corbis: 11bl.
Harmut Schwarzbach/Rex Features: 28b. Sipa-Press/Rex Features: 10bl, 21b.
Jon Spaul/The Refugee Council: 18t. Sporting Pictures: 28-29.
Liba Taylor/Panos Pictures: 19b. David Tothill/Photofusion: 14b, 17b.
Wilhemsen/Rex Features 16t. Philip Wolmuth/Panos Pictures: 7t.

CONTENTS

Whenever we pass through an airport, an immigration officer checks our passport to see if we are allowed to enter the country.

OVER THE PAST DECADE, *more and more people have migrated to the developed world, both legally and illegally. These migrants, often of different race and colour, are seen as a threat to Western economies and culture. Governments have spent billions of dollars on tightening their borders. Immigration and asylum are two of the most talked about issues in the news today.*

A WORLD ON THE MOVE

Immigration does not only affect developed countries. There are an estimated 150 million people who live abroad as immigrants in countries all over the world. Air travel, better communication, global trade, but also war, conflicts, famine and natural disasters have increased the number of people on the move around the world.

LEGAL IMMIGRATION

Governments in the developed world have very strict immigration laws. Immigrants can usually only apply to join close family members already in the country. Some countries, including Australia but not those in Western Europe, allow a limited number of foreigners to come and work if they have special skills or talents. This is called special skills migration. Most travellers abroad are simply visitors.

IMMIGRATION CONTROL

Immigration control is designed to allow only those people with valid travel and identity documentation into the country. Embassies can refuse to issue visas to people from countries that produce large numbers of illegal immigrants or asylum seekers. Airlines and other companies are also required to check whether passengers have the right documentation and can refuse to carry them.

ILLEGAL IMMIGRATION

Stricter immigration control means fewer people manage to obtain visas to get to a developed country. In poorer countries, people may have difficulty obtaining passports from their own government or they may need special permission to travel abroad. People with few or no skills have virtually no chance of emigrating legally to developed countries. Their only option is to emigrate illegally.

⬇ *Police and border officials in developed countries have the power to stop and arrest suspected illegal immigrants.*

GET THE FACTS STRAIGHT

Here are some definitions of key words in the immigration debate:

- **Immigration:** the process of people arriving at, and passing through, border controls in a foreign country.
- **Asylum:** an immigration status given to people who fear serious persecution in their home country.
- **Emigrant:** a person who has decided to leave home and country for good.
- **Immigrant:** someone allowed to come into a foreign country to settle.
- **Illegal immigrant:** someone who has entered a foreign country without permission but wants to settle there.
- **Migrant:** a person moving from one place or country to another to find short- or longer-term work.
- **Visitor:** a visitor is someone who has permission to go abroad and returns after a short period of time.

MIGRATION IS NOT *a new process. It often results in economic development. Several hundred years ago, as European explorers settled in other continents like North America and Australia, they brought knowledge and technology with them. They built an economy and so attracted more immigrants to come and join in their new life.*

ECONOMIC DEVELOPMENT AND IMMIGRATION

People in developed countries earn more money doing skilled work and are less inclined to do work that does not require special skills. This provides an opportunity for people from poorer countries to come to the developed world to take on this work. They are able to earn far more money much more quickly than they ever could in their own country. As they work hard and start to earn money, they begin to improve their quality of life and may encourage family and friends to come and join them.

Leaving your country is a big step to take. Before you consider some specific concerns about immigration and asylum, you might want to think about and discuss these questions:

- Can you think of reasons that could make you decide to emigrate?
- What risks would you take if you emigrated? Would you be prepared to do so illegally?
- How important would it be for you to be able to return to your country?
- How would you feel if you were unable to return to your country?

European immigrants enter the United States through Ellis Island in New York City, 1907. They went there in search of new opportunities and wealth.

Immigrants provide a large, unskilled workforce – vital for many industries in the developed world, such as this mail-order company.

ECONOMIC DEVELOPMENT AND EMIGRATION

Most developed countries are not just countries of immigration but also emigration. More and more of their skilled workers and professionals move to other developed countries to further their career or because their company sends them. Some countries, like Italy and Ireland, now see many people who emigrated to Australia or North America years ago returning to their homeland.

ECONOMIC DEVELOPMENT AND ILLEGAL IMMIGRATION

Economic development around the world needs workers. Large companies do not only recruit local workers but also need workers in offices and factories set up in other countries. As more and more companies invest money in countries where labour is cheap, those countries themselves start to develop and need workers. The modern world encourages free trade but immigration policies still very much restrict the free movement of workers. Many companies depend on illegal migrants and immigrants.

SINCE THE 1950s, *several million people have been given asylum worldwide. Today, over 1.2 million asylum applications are awaiting official decisions. Increased mobility has resulted in more asylum seekers in developed countries, especially in Western Europe during the 1990s.*

WHAT IS ASYLUM?

Asylum literally means safe haven. After the Second World War, asylum became a legal immigration status in developed countries. This status is given to people who have fled their home and country because of persecution. Most developed countries have set up complicated asylum procedures to help them decide whether someone should get asylum or not. Asylum is also called refugee status.

WHO IS A REFUGEE?

The 1951 United Nations Convention Relating to the Status of Refugees, an international legal document, defines a refugee as someone who has a well-founded fear of persecution for reasons of race, religion, nationality, membership of a particular social group or political opinion. Under the Convention, people fleeing famine or natural disasters are not refugees.

Kosovar refugees arrive at Leeds airport in the UK in 1999 to find protection from persecution in Kosovo.

ARE ASYLUM SEEKERS REFUGEES?

In developed countries, people who apply for asylum are called asylum seekers. They have to wait and see whether they are recognised as a refugee or not. However, the majority of people fleeing danger do not apply for asylum because they end up in poorer countries in the Middle East and Africa. A tiny percentage of them are allowed to resettle in a small number of developed countries, including Australia.

THE IMPORTANCE OF ASYLUM

Asylum is a fundamental human right as set out in the 1948 Universal Declaration of Human Rights. There are over 40 wars and conflicts in the world today. Many governments today do not respect human rights. One hundred and thirty-nine countries including Australia, Canada, the United Kingdom and the United States have signed the 1951 Convention and committed themselves to protecting refugees.

A refugee family starts a new life in Germany. Most refugees have to leave their families behind.

BETWEEN 1990 AND 2000, about 12,000 people were found to be illegal immigrants in Australia. At the same time, Australia received about 90,000 asylum applications. There are more than five million illegal immigrants in the United States where there were about 900,000 asylum applications from 1990 to 2000.

GET THE FACTS STRAIGHT

These were the countries with the most asylum applications in 2000, according to UNHCR.

Country	Asylum applications
● Germany:	117, 648
● United States:	91,454
● United Kingdom:	75,680
● The Netherlands:	43,895
● Belgium:	42,691
● Switzerland:	32,434
● Italy:	14,000

ILLEGAL IMMIGRANT OR ASYLUM SEEKER?

Many people in the developed world think all asylum seekers are illegal immigrants. They are not. Many come as visitors and then apply for asylum. Others apply immediately on arrival in the new country. Equally, not all illegal immigrants become asylum seekers. People who flee persecution may be afraid to approach authorities in a foreign country. People who come to work and arrive illegally often only apply for asylum if the immigration authorities find them.

⬅ *Millions of people from Afghanistan have embarked on a difficult journey to cross the border into Pakistan. Some try to travel still further and seek asylum in the developed world.*

Asylum-seeking children often find it difficult to adjust to school life in a new country and learning in a new language.

Asylum seekers queue to use a phone in a special detention facility. They may not have known that they could be detained when they claimed asylum.

WHY DO PEOPLE APPLY FOR ASYLUM?

Some are in danger back home and want safety for themselves and their family. Others are forced to seek a better life abroad because the political and economic situation in their country does not allow them to earn a living. They claim asylum for stability and security in their lives, but normally do not qualify for asylum. Others simply want to work and may not even be aware that they have no chance of passing the asylum test in a developed country.

WHY DON'T THEY GO ELSEWHERE?

Asylum seekers may have specific reasons for coming to a particular country. They may have family, friends or an established community there. Language is often a factor. The asylum country may have historic ties with the asylum seeker's own country. Many asylum seekers get someone else to arrange the journey for them and have little choice about the destination country.

MOST WESTERN GOVERNMENTS have signed the 1951 Convention on Refugees and are responsible for protecting recognised refugees. But as more people have sought asylum in recent years, governments have responded by tightening immigration control, providing minimum support to destitute asylum seekers, and applying stricter criteria for giving asylum. As a result, the percentage of applicants granted asylum has steadily decreased.

IMMIGRATION CONTROL BEFORE ARRIVAL

As more asylum seekers arrive, governments try to find ways to discourage people from setting out to apply for asylum in the first place. They increase checks at airports abroad. To deter visitors applying for asylum, they also impose visa restrictions on countries that produce significant numbers of asylum seekers.

DETENTION

Western governments have increasingly used detention as a means to stop asylum seekers from coming. Asylum seekers in Australia who arrive illegally are always detained. The United Kingdom detains both newly arrived and unsuccessful asylum seekers in prisons and detention centres across the country and aims to house more asylum seekers in reception centres in the future, where asylum seekers will not be allowed to come and go freely.

GET THE FACTS STRAIGHT

The amount of support a government gives asylum seekers is constantly under review:

- Australia: asylum seekers who come to Australia legally and apply for asylum within 45 days receive Medicare assistance and may be entitled to some income support after six months. They can apply for permission to work.

- United Kingdom: asylum seekers can apply for food vouchers and pocket money given out weekly, amounting to 69% of income support levels. This voucher support system is costly and difficult to implement, so there are plans to abolish it and keep asylum seekers in designated reception centres instead. Asylum seekers can apply for work permission within six months of the date of their asylum application.

- United States: asylum seekers can only apply for work permission 150 days after their arrival. They have access to limited support, medical help and food stamps. Charities usually help them.

MINIMUM SUPPORT

Many governments provide little or no support to asylum seekers, especially those who arrive illegally. Some governments, like Germany or the United Kingdom, have changed asylum legislation several times during the 1990s to reduce the amount of support asylum seekers can get. Governments believe that limited support will dissuade more people from coming and applying for asylum.

⬇ *Hungary has recently turned open community shelters into closed detention centres to be able to detain more asylum seekers .*

DILEMMA

Governments are in a dilemma. On the one hand they are committed to protecting people in danger. At the same time they are responsible for immigration control. The number of people seeking to get to the West is unlikely to decrease if poorer countries do not become politically and economically more stable. Many people in developed countries, however, fear that more immigrants and asylum seekers will be a threat to their own national identity.

ONE OF THE MAIN REASONS why people talk about immigrants and asylum seekers in a negative way is the belief that they come to live off welfare benefits. However, governments have imposed strict conditions on immigrants who want to come to work or be with their family and they do not give them access to benefits.

⬇ *A Kosovar asylum seeker is waiting for a decision on his asylum application.*

FACING THE ISSUES

Abdul sought asylum in Britain when he was nine. He is now 14 and is still waiting for a decision on his status. His parents were murdered during clan fighting in Somalia. Abdul was found clinging to his mother's body. He and his brother were cared for by an aunt who brought them to the United Kingdom. Eventually due to poverty and stress the aunt was no longer able to care for her nephews as well as her own children. Abdul was taken into foster care along with his brother. In school, Abdul has been exposed to extremely cruel verbal abuse about his mother. As a result, he often becomes involved in fights and has been suspended from school several times. [Source: Save the Children, UK]

WHAT ASYLUM SEEKERS LIVE ON

Governments in the developed world have different ways of supporting asylum seekers who are destitute. Asylum seekers are either not entitled to mainstream welfare benefits or receive a reduced amount, often only for the first few months after their arrival. In some countries, asylum seekers get food vouchers and small amounts of money for essential items or are supported in reception centres. Asylum seekers who are detained are not given any money.

LIVING IN LIMBO

Some governments have recently focused their efforts on speeding up decisions on asylum applications. Asylum seekers in the UK used to wait up to ten years for a decision. Now it takes a few months. The Australian Government takes a minimum of 15 weeks to decide on asylum applications in detention centres. Because many asylum applications are being refused more quickly, more appeals against refusals are being lodged. These days, asylum seekers who appeal often have to wait several years for a final decision.

RACIAL HARASSMENT

Most governments disperse asylum seekers to different parts of the country and house them where accommodation is available. This tends to be in poor, isolated areas away from town centres and where there are higher levels of unemployment. Such areas make asylum seekers an easy target for racial attacks. Some have even been killed.

Many asylum seekers are housed on run-down 'sink' estates and are easy targets for racial abuse.

MANY ILLEGAL IMMIGRANTS *undertake difficult journeys to get to the West. Those wishing to apply for asylum face further problems.*

DANGEROUS JOURNEYS

In June 2000, 58 Chinese illegal immigrants were found dead in the back of a lorry by immigration authorities at the port of Dover in the United Kingdom. Hundreds of people are thought to have drowned trying to reach Australia by boat. German border guards regularly find dead illegal immigrants in the rivers along its border with Poland.

ARRIVAL

Most developed-world governments believe that people who immediately apply for asylum on arrival or while they are in the country legally are more likely to be refugees than those who arrive illegally. In Australia, all asylum seekers who come in as illegal immigrants are sent to detention centres. European countries do not admit people who have travelled through other safe countries into their asylum procedure.

⬆ *In 2001, the Australian Government refused to let these Afghans land and so denied them the chance to apply for asylum.*

⬇ *Chinese illegal immigrants trying to cross the Channel to reach the United Kingdom are caught by French police.*

THE ASYLUM APPLICATION

Applying for asylum involves completing a long, complicated asylum application form in the language of the asylum country. Asylum seekers need to be precise about the reasons why they think they should get asylum. They need to know the 1951 Convention. Most don't and they need legal advice. But many asylum seekers are interviewed within days of arrival. They have not had time to find a lawyer. Detained asylum seekers may not always be told that they are entitled to legal advice.

SUCCESSFUL?

In recent years, about 23% of asylum applicants in Australia have been given asylum compared to 24% in the UK. Some countries (but not Australia) give unsuccessful applicants a form of humanitarian status if they do not meet the refugee criteria of the 1951 Convention, but would still be in danger if they were returned home. Asylum seekers can normally appeal if their asylum application is refused. Some appeals are successful.

➡ *This Kosovar asylum seeker is keen to learn English to make a new start.*

WHAT DO YOU THINK?

Have you followed the news on TV recently? Or seen any newspaper headlines about asylum seekers in your local or national newspaper? Collect some newspaper cuttings about asylum seekers and read them carefully to answer the following questions:

- Were the stories mostly negative or positive?
- If they were negative, what was it that made them negative?
- If they were positive, what positive aspects did they mention about asylum seekers?
- Do stories in the newspapers about asylum seekers affect the way you think about them?

ASYLUM SEEKERS ONLY *get asylum if they can show that they are personally in serious danger and would be persecuted by their government if they were returned. To establish this, they have to give credible and consistent statements and provide personal evidence. At the same time, the authorities have to be convinced that the human rights situation in the asylum seeker's country of origin is bad.*

This man fled Iraq. He was given asylum as he could prove his life was in danger if he returned to his own country. He still protests about Iraq's ruler, Saddam Hussein.

WHO DOES NOT GET ASYLUM?

The majority of asylum seekers come from countries that are politically unstable or run by totalitarian regimes. An unstable political situation often leads to a country's economy breaking down so many asylum seekers flee political and economic insecurity at the same time. They do not meet the 1951 Convention definition and will not get asylum. Asylum seekers fleeing war or civil war situations often do not qualify for asylum, as they cannot prove fear of individual persecution. In these cases, some governments may decide to allow them to stay on humanitarian grounds.

WHO GETS ASYLUM?

Asylum seekers from Afghanistan, Somalia, Iraq and Iran are currently most likely to succeed with their asylum application. However, different governments have slightly different ways of interpreting the 1951 Convention. An asylum application given refugee status in one country may be refused or only given humanitarian status in another.

WHO ARE ECONOMIC MIGRANTS?

Economic migrants are people who move to another country intending to work. Most economic migrants to developed countries come from other developed countries. In the United Kingdom, there are about 400,000 migrants from other European Union countries. They come for better salaries and work experience.

Asylum seekers by definition are people who want to be considered as refugees under the 1951 Convention. There are no statistics on the number of asylum seekers whose main motive for being in a country is to work and who are only applying for asylum to stay there legally. Many illegal immigrants who come to work will risk living and working illegally rather than applying for asylum and so making themselves known to the authorities.

🔽 *A Cambodian who was granted asylum at work. Not all refugees are able to use their skills and qualifications obtained back home in their new country.*

GET THE FACTS STRAIGHT

In 2000, 7% of all asylum seekers were given asylum in developed countries. These statistics from UNHCR show that of this 7%, the most successful asylum seekers came from the following countries:

- Iraq (11%)
- Former Yugoslavia (9%)
- Somalia (8%)

And these statistics show how the success of asylum seekers from those three countries were around the world:

- **Australia:** Former Yugoslavia 44%; Iraq 90%; Somalia 39%
- **France:** Former Yugoslavia 23%; Iraq 47%; Somalia 65%
- **Germany:** Former Yugoslavia 1%; Iraq 58%; Somalia 0%
- **United Kingdom:** Former Yugoslavia 2%; Iraq 16%; Somalia 48%
- **United States:** Former Yugoslavia 40%; Iraq 74%; Somalia 60%

WORKING ILLEGALLY

ILLEGAL WORKERS ARE NOT

necessarily illegal immigrants. An illegal worker may have permission to be in the country but not be allowed to work or claim benefits - for example students or tourists. Asylum seekers are allowed to stay in the country until a decision on their asylum claim is made but are often not allowed to work. There are an estimated 15 to 30 million people thought to work illegally around the world.

⊕ Illegal workers are usually paid on a daily basis in cash. Some may find they get less than they were promised.

WHAT DO YOU THINK?

- How do you react to stories of illegal immigrants in your local newspaper?
- Why do you think you react in this way?
- What do you think are the main reasons for people wanting to risk their lives to migrate?
- Do you think governments in developed countries are right to control immigration?
- What do you think would happen if immigration control did not exist?

WHY WORK ILLEGALLY?

If people can stay in their chosen country but cannot work and have no money of their own, they may risk working illegally to make ends meet. Many people who have arrived illegally and had their journey arranged by an agent, owe a lot of money to the agent. They work illegally not only to survive but to pay back the money they owe.

WHERE ARE ILLEGAL WORKERS?

People working illegally do not want to be found out and try to stay as invisible as they can. Illegal workers are usually forced to work hard, long hours and often perform physically demanding work. They may work on building sites, as painters and decorators, in hotels and restaurants, on farms, as drivers or cleaners.

Illegal workers are usually poorly paid. Sometimes they may not get paid at all after a few days' work and have to move on to find other work. As they work illegally, they have no rights and cannot rely on protection from trade unions and government laws. They may have to pay money to their employer for food and accommodation.

WHO ELSE BENEFITS?

People who employ illegal workers benefit because they do not have to spend as much money on salaries or any money on holiday or sick pay. People who are involved in helping illegal workers find work and providing them with false work permits benefit, as these services are usually quite expensive. The public benefits because illegal workers often do work which locals would not do!

⬇ *This American clothes factory is close to the Mexican border and depends on illegal migrants from Mexico.*

Bury College
Learning Resources
Woodbury Centre

THE TRAGEDY OF THE 58 Chinese illegal immigrants found dead in a lorry at Dover (see page 16) shocked the world. In August 2001, a group of Romanians were found hiding in the undercarriage of a Eurostar train as it arrived in London from Brussels. But new smuggling routes are established all the time. As long as people migrate illegally, they will turn to smugglers for help.

⬆ *The personal effects of an immigrant who died trying to reach the West. They include a picture of US film star Leonardo di Caprio.*

SMUGGLED

As most immigrants from less developed countries have no chance of finding legal ways to get into developed countries, they increasingly turn to illegal methods. In particular, they pay agents, known as smugglers, huge sums of money to arrange false travel documents, transportation and help in crossing borders.

FACING THE ISSUES

Viktor is a 22-year old from Montenegro who went to the United Kingdom and claimed asylum. He paid £500 to a smuggling ring to get there. His application was rejected. He now gets no support and is not allowed to work. He is forced to work illegally doing any job he can get. [Source: *The Guardian*]

TRAFFICKED

Smuggling immigrants into the West can lead to exploitation. Many immigrants, especially women and children, pay to be smuggled but are then forced into prostitution or begging either by agents or connected criminal groups. They are trafficked. Their smugglers are called traffickers. A huge number of women and children are trafficked around the world each year – an estimated 700,000 across US borders alone.

➡ *Eastern European women are often forced by their own families to go begging with their child.*

CHEAP LABOUR

Immigrants smuggled into the West pay a lot of money to smugglers. They pay before they travel and, once they are in the West, they still owe their smugglers thousands of dollars. They are desperate to work and have to accept work that is usually paid very little money – well below the minimum wage of the country.

Once immigrants manage to pay off their debts, they work hard and send most of what they earn back home to their families. In 1998, an estimated $52.8 billion dollars earned by migrants abroad were sent back to their countries. Western governments only gave about half that amount in aid to poorer countries.

THERE IS A PERCEPTION in the West that countries cannot cope with the arrival of any more immigrants and asylum seekers. But there are also many people leaving developed countries. Some emigrate for a different life or a career move; some return home after spending time abroad. Rich countries will soon need more immigrants to maintain essential services.

NOT ENOUGH

In Western countries, people have fewer children. They also live longer than was the case a few decades ago. This means that in the future there will be more people above working age, but not enough people working and bringing in money to support the rest of the population. In Japan and Europe, the population is expected to decline. In Canada, the United States and Australia, the population is expected to grow slightly, but they will also be short of people of working age.

⬇ *The need for workers in the West gives whole immigrant families an opportunity to earn money.*

This Asian radio presenter is making her mark in the media world.

WHAT DO GOVERNMENTS DO?

In the 1960s and 1970s, Western governments admitted thousands of guest-workers from non-European countries to work for a fixed period. This is happening again. Canada has set up a guest-worker programme for Mexicans. The United States plans to do the same. Germany and the United Kingdom have started to change their immigration rules to allow people with special skills, such as doctors, IT experts and teachers, into their country. Australia also encourages professionals to immigrate.

THE FUTURE

Some people think that the European Union alone needs almost a million migrants to stop the population from declining. During the 1990s, only just over 800,000 people migrated to Europe. There is a trend for professionals from non-Western countries who immigrate to spend less time in the West and return back to their country after only a few years. This means that Western countries continue to need a more flexible approach to immigration to ensure there are enough people of working age in the future.

GET THE FACTS STRAIGHT

These are the United Nation's estimates of population trends in top industrialised countries:

Country	1950	2000	2015	2050
Australia	8,219,000	19,138,000	21,910,000	26,502,000
Canada	13,737,000	30,757,000	34,419,000	40,407,000
Germany	68,378,000	82,017,000	80,673,000	70,805,000
United Kingdom	50,616,000	59,415,000	60,566,000	58,933,000
United States	157,813,000	283,230,000	321,225,000	397,063,000

IMMIGRANTS CAN FIND IT difficult to adapt to life in a new country: a new language, a new climate, different food and different systems. Most immigrants come from very different cultural and religious backgrounds. They may be of different colour. They often stick with people from their own community to feel secure.

RISE IN RACISM

Recently racial attacks against asylum seekers in developed countries have increased. Asylum seekers, unlike illegal immigrants or immigrants who have established themselves, have become more noticeable to the local population. Newly arrived, they have few possessions, do not speak the language and are dependent on government support. This can cause resentment, especially if the asylum seekers are housed in poorer areas of the country not used to seeing foreigners.

RACISM AND THE MEDIA

Racism does not just affect asylum seekers. It can affect already established immigrant groups. In 2001, there were bad race riots in the north of England between Asian and white British young people. Unemployment and lack of economic investment are the main reasons. Some people feel race issues are made worse by newspapers, which claim that the arrival of foreigners is a threat to the culture and economy of the country and call for tighter immigration controls.

Race riots in poorer areas in some West European countries have become a worrying feature in recent years.

IMMIGRANT FOREVER?

Immigrants who have lived many years in a new country may not see themselves as immigrants any longer. Some refugees feel strongly about their identity as refugee, others may prefer to forget why they became refugees in the first place. Immigrants, who have become citizens and identify themselves with their new home country, may begin to resent having to share their success with other immigrants who have arrived more recently.

← *Many refugees who have been forced to flee would prefer to return to their country if it was safe enough for them.*

↓ *Governments usually take pride in the fact that their society is multicultural.*

WHAT DO YOU THINK?

In most countries, racial harassment or racial attacks are recognised as crimes.

- Do you think it is right to link asylum issues with racism?
- What kind of actions do you think would be called racial harassment?
- Have you heard or witnessed racial harassment at school or in your area?
- What would you do if you heard someone say something racist about someone you know?
- How does your local newspaper deal with racial issues?

IMMIGRATION CONTROL HAS ONLY

existed for a little over a hundred years. At the time, Western countries became so-called sovereign countries. Sovereignty is about controlling your own affairs and establishing a national identity. The term 'immigrant' only describes the initial process of immigrating. In terms of identity, an immigrant is still a national of his home country.

⊗ *Many people hold dual nationality – they are citizens of two different countries, but only resident in one.*

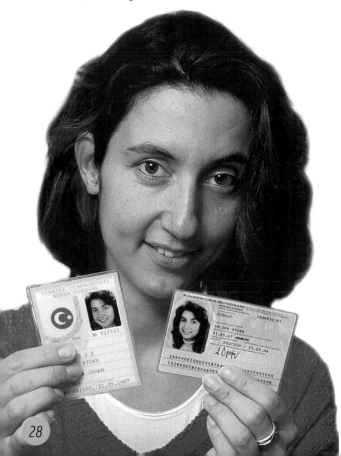

⊕ *Pole-vaulter Dimitri Markov is a native of Belarus but became an Australian citizen. He won a gold medal for his new country in the World Athletic Championships in 2001.*

CITIZENSHIP

As a citizen you have rights and responsibilities. Citizenship means you are entitled to vote in elections. You can yourself be elected into local or national government. You are entitled to a passport and you can count on your government for help and protection when you are abroad. As a citizen you also commit yourself to the laws and values of your country.

These are all different terms for people's status in a country.

- Alien: some countries like Taiwan and the United States use the term 'alien' as a formal description for foreigner.
- Foreigner: the most commonly used term for describing people who come from other countries. It is not an official immigration term.
- Resident: residents are people who are living legally in a foreign country and have no conditions set on their stay. They are normally entitled to welfare benefits and are able to vote in local but not necessarily national elections.
- National: people are nationals of the country they are born in. This means they are normally also automatically citizens of that country.
- Citizen: citizens of a country are not necessarily nationals but have gained citizenship after they have been in the country legally for some time.

ARE IMMIGRANTS CITIZENS?

Immigrants do not have an automatic right to citizenship, but they can apply to become a citizen. They have to meet many conditions to succeed. They must speak the language. They must show that they have lived in the country legally for many years. They must know the history and culture of the country. Most countries do not allow people to hold two nationalities, so some immigrants may have to give up their original nationality to become a citizen of their new home country.

ARE ASYLUM SEEKERS CITIZENS?

Asylum seekers wait to see if the government recognises them as refugees. If they get refugee status, they can live in the country without any conditions but still have to apply for citizenship like any other immigrant. For refugees, national identity is an issue because they have effectively given up their original nationality by seeking protection from another government. If they return home, they will lose their refugee status. Most refugees hope eventually to become citizens of the country that has given them asylum.

GLOSSARY

aid: Money or support given to countries in need by governments and charities.

asylum: A special legal immigration status given to people who are recognised as refugees according to the 1951 Convention on Refugees.

asylum appeal: If an asylum application is rejected by the authorities, asylum seekers can appeal to have the decision overturned.

asylum seekers: People seeking a special legal status called asylum or refugee status to stay in another country because they fear persecution at home.

citizen: A person who has a legal right to live in a country, vote for its government and is protected by its laws. It is possible to become a citizen of a country even if you were born elsewhere.

Convention Relating to the Status of Refugees (1951): The key international agreement drafted by the United Nations, which defines the term 'refugee' and obliges countries who have signed up to it to protect refugees.

destitute: People who have no home or access to money.

detention centres: Secure buildings used by some developed countries to contain asylum seekers whilst their applications are considered.

economic migrants: People who move to a country intending to work there.

guest-workers: People from less wealthy countries who are invited to work in a developed country for a limited period of time to fill specific jobs.

humanitarian status: When a person is allowed to stay in a country on humanitarian grounds, because it would be dangerous for them to return home, although that person does not legally qualify for asylum.

immigration: The process of people arriving at, and passing through, border controls in a foreign country.

income support: Money given by a government to help people on low salaries.

migration: The movement of people from one area or country to another in search of work or a different life-style.

minimum wage: The lowest legally acceptable hourly wage set by a government.

racial harrassment: Abusing people of other ethnic groups, such as by verbal threats or attacks on their property.

refugees: People who flee their country, seek asylum elsewhere and are recognised as refugees under international law.

trade unions: Organisations devoted to campaigning for fair rights for workers.

traffickers: People who smuggle illegal immigrants for a sum of money and then force them to work for them, often as prostitutes or beggars.

Universal Declaration of Human Rights (1948): An internationally agreed set of rights to which every person in the world is entitled. They include, among many things, the right to free speech, education, and to seek and enjoy asylum from persecution in other countries.

visa: Stamp on a passport to show that its bearer has been given permission to visit a country by embassy officials from that country.

welfare benefits: Help or money given by a government to people who are on low incomes, do not have access to decent housing, are suffering an illness or are unemployed.

FURTHER INFORMATION

INTERNATIONAL ORGANISATIONS

International Organisation for Migration (IOM)
www.iom.int
Comprehensive information on migration issues worldwide.

United Nations (UN)
www.un.org
The Population Department link has information about global population statistics and trends.

United Nations High Commissioner for Refugees (UNHCR)
www.unhcr.ch
The site has comprehensive information on basic refugee issues, refugee statistics, news from refugee-producing countries, and a list of UNHCR offices worldwide.

NON-GOVERNMENTAL ORGANISATIONS

Anti-Slavery International
www.antislavery.org
Oldest international human rights organisation set up in 1839 to campaign against slavery and forced labour. Has useful information about trafficking.

Australian Refugee Council
www.refugeecouncil.org.au
Comprehensive information on asylum issues and statistics in Australia.

British Refugee Council
www.refugeecouncil.org.uk
Largest refugee charity in the UK based in London.

Canadian Council for Refugees
www.web.net/~ccr
Information on refugees' rights, asylum procedures and integration issues in Canada.

Electronic Immigration Network
www.ein.org.uk
Project based in Manchester, UK, providing on-line information on asylum appeal cases. Has excellent links to other websites worldwide.

European Council on Refugees and Exiles
www.ecre.org
Covers law and policy issues in the European refugee and asylum field. Has a Europe-wide membership base.

National Immigration Forum
www.immigrationforum.org
An independent US body which aims to build positive public support for immigrants and refugees.

Pro-Asyl
www.proasyl.de
Campaigns for asylum seekers' rights in Germany and Europe-wide. Site is translated into English.

The US Committee for Refugees
www.refugees.org
US refugee agency. The site has comprehensive information on global refugee issues, country information and global statistics.

GOVERNMENT SITES

Australian Department of Immigration and Multicultural Affairs
www.immi.gov.au

Citizenship and Immigration Canada
www.cic.gc.ca

United Kingdom Home Office Immigration and Nationality Directorate
www.ind.homeoffice.gov.uk

United States Immigration and Naturalization Service
www.ins.usdoj.gov

INDEX